MICHAEL DAUGHERTY
VENETIAN BLINDS

FOR SOLO PIANO
(2002)

HENDON MUSIC

BOOSEY & HAWKES

AN IMAGEM COMPANY

DISTRIBUTED BY

HAL•LEONARD®
CORPORATION
7777 W. BLUEMOUND RD. P.O. BOX 13819 MILWAUKEE, WI 53213

www.boosey.com
www.halleonard.com

Published by Boosey & Hawkes, Inc.
229 West 28th Street, 11th Floor
New York NY 10001

www.boosey.com

AN IMAGEM COMPANY

ISMN 979-0-051-24645-8

Photography:
Cover: *Nighthawk* (1943) Courtesy of Shorpy. Used by permission.
Preliminary text: *Out of the Past* (1947). Public Domain

First printed 2013
Music engraving by Paul Dooley and Patrick Harlin

Commissioned by La Biennale di Venezia

First performance by Mauro Castellano, piano,
La Biennale di Venezia, September 28, 2002

BIOGRAPHY

Michael Daugherty is one of the most commissioned, performed, and recorded composers on the American concert music scene today. His music is rich with cultural allusions and bears the stamp of classic modernism, with colliding tonalities and blocks of sound; at the same time, his melodies can be eloquent and stirring. Daugherty has been hailed by *The Times* (London) as "a master icon maker" with a "maverick imagination, fearless structural sense and meticulous ear." Daugherty first came to international attention when the Baltimore Symphony Orchestra, conducted by David Zinman, performed his *Metropolis Symphony* at Carnegie Hall in 1994. Since that time, Daugherty's music has entered the orchestral, band and chamber music repertory and made him, according to the League of American Orchestras, one of the ten most performed American composers.

In 2011, the Nashville Symphony's Naxos recording of Daugherty's *Metropolis Symphony* and *Deus ex Machina* was honored with three GRAMMY® Awards, including Best Classical Contemporary Composition.

Born in 1954 in Cedar Rapids, Iowa, Daugherty is the son of a dance-band drummer and the oldest of five brothers, all professional musicians. He studied music composition at the University of North Texas (1972-76), the Manhattan School of Music (1976-78), and computer music at Pierre Boulez's IRCAM in Paris (1979-80). Daugherty received his doctorate from Yale University in 1986 where his teachers included Jacob Druckman, Earle Brown, Roger Reynolds, and Bernard Rands. During this time, he also collaborated with jazz arranger Gil Evans in New York, and pursued further studies with composer György Ligeti in Hamburg, Germany (1982-84). After teaching music composition from 1986-90 at the Oberlin Conservatory of Music, Daugherty joined the School of Music at the University of Michigan (Ann Arbor) in 1991, where he is Professor of Composition and a mentor to many of today's most talented young composers.

Daugherty has been Composer-in-Residence with the Louisville Symphony Orchestra (2000), Detroit Symphony Orchestra (1999-2003), Colorado Symphony Orchestra (2001-02), Cabrillo Festival of Contemporary Music (2001-04, 2006-08, 2011), Westshore Symphony Orchestra (2005-06), Eugene Symphony (2006), Henry Mancini Summer Institute (2006), Music from Angel Fire Chamber Music Festival (2006), Pacific Symphony (2010-11), Chattanooga Symphony (2012-13) and New Century Chamber Orchestra (2013).

Daugherty has received numerous awards, distinctions, and fellowships for his music, including: a Fulbright Fellowship (1977), the Kennedy Center Friedheim Award (1989), the Goddard Lieberson Fellowship from the American Academy of Arts and Letters (1991), fellowships from the National Endowment for the Arts (1992) and the Guggenheim Foundation (1996), and the Stoeger Prize from the Chamber Music Society of Lincoln Center (2000). In 2005, Daugherty received the Lancaster Symphony Orchestra Composer's Award, and in 2007, the Delaware Symphony Orchestra selected Daugherty as the winner of the A.I. DuPont Award. Also in 2007, he received the American Bandmasters Association Ostwald Award for his composition *Raise the Roof* for Timpani and Symphonic Band. Daugherty has been named "Outstanding Classical Composer" at the Detroit Music Awards in 2007, 2009 and 2010. His GRAMMY® award winning recordings can be heard on Albany, Argo, Delos, Equilibrium, Klavier, Naxos and Nonesuch labels.

Robert Mitchum, as the doomed hero, and Jane Greer, as the femme fatale
in the film noir classic *Out of the Past* (1947)

COMPOSER'S NOTE

Venetian Blinds (2002) for Solo Piano was commissioned by La Biennale di Venezia and first performed by Mauro Castellano, piano, at La Biennale di Venezia on September, 28, 2002 in Venice, Italy. The work is 9 minutes in duration and divided into three movements: Dark, Shadows, and Light.

In *Venetian Blinds*, I evoke different musical moods associated with classic American film noir cinema produced at the RKO Hollywood studios such as *Out of the Past* (1947) starring Robert Mitchum (1917-1997). Incorporating complex plots full of double-crossing and betrayal by hoodlums, hard boiled detectives, doomed heroes and femmes fatales, these black and white films created an ambiguous and mysterious atmosphere of darkness, shadow and light.

In film noir, Venetian blinds were often used to create an interplay of shadows by adjusting the angle of the blind slats in order to control how much light entered a room on the movie set. My composition uses Venetian blinds as a metaphor to control the amount of darkness and light we hear from the piano. The three movements of *Venetian Blinds* are contrasting episodes of musical intrigue and suspense.

The first movement (Dark) explores the deep, dark undercurrents of the piano keyboard. The music is sleepy, murky, bluesy, and chords voiced as dense note clusters allow little light. In the second movement (Shadows) we hear glissandi racing up and down the piano keyboard like slats on half-opened Venetian blinds; the alternation of black and white keys creates sharp contrast and sometimes the hands of the pianist cross over like a double-crossing film noir plot. The final movement (Light) is a musical flashback, with flashes of radiant, pulsating energy. The chords are bright and widely spaced, and the hands are separated to evoke a feeling of lightness and openness. Intricate musical patterns and dramatic juxtaposition of timbre and dynamics recreate the black and white drama of American film noir cinema.

—Michael Daugherty

commissioned by the Venice Biennale

VENETIAN BLINDS

I. Dark

Piano part edited by
Andrea Rebaudengo

MICHAEL DAUGHERTY
(2002)

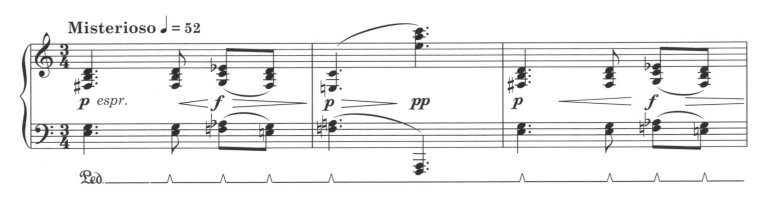

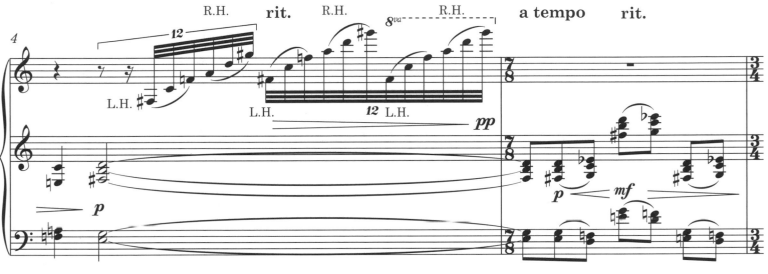

979-0-051-24645-8

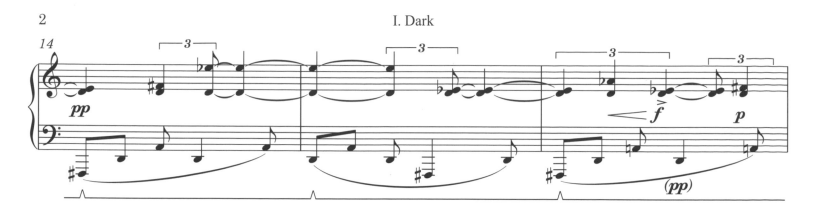

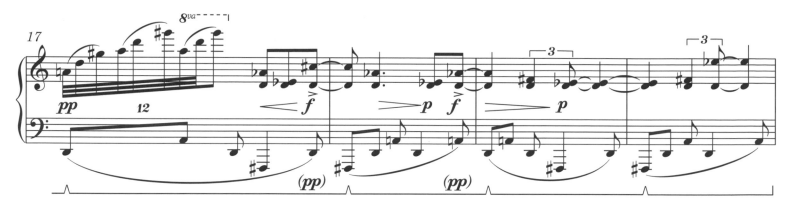

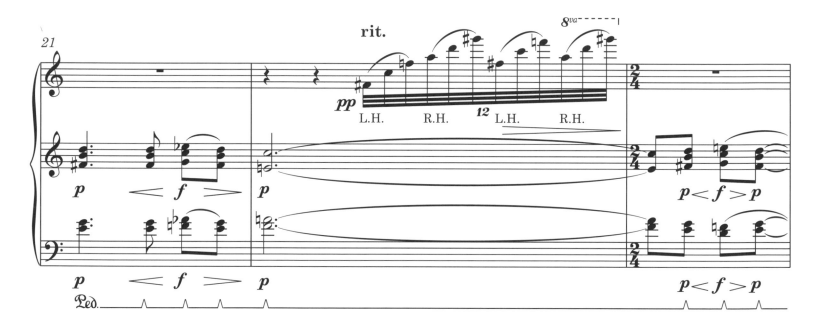

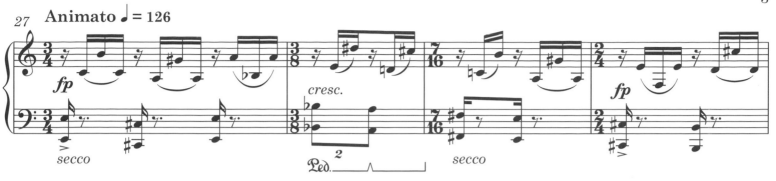

Misterioso ♩ = 52

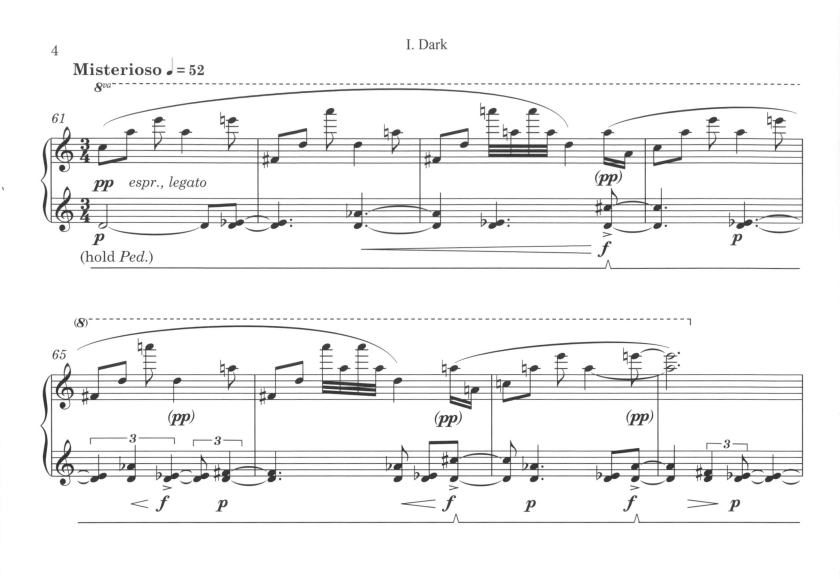

Blank
for turn

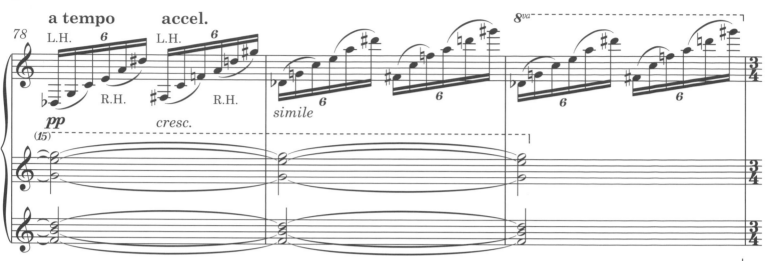

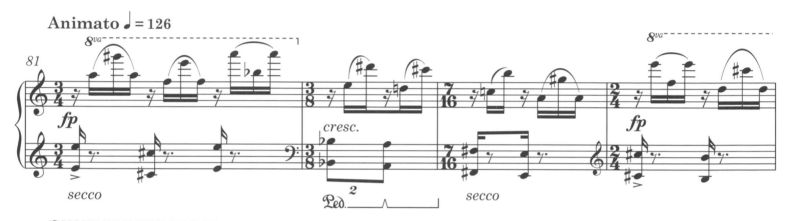

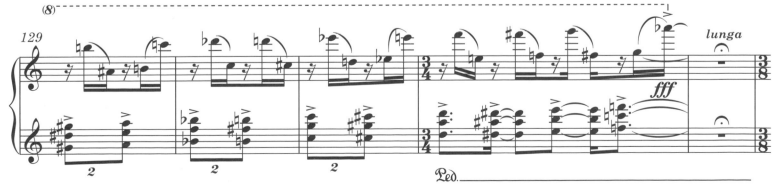

I. Dark

Misterioso ♩ = 52

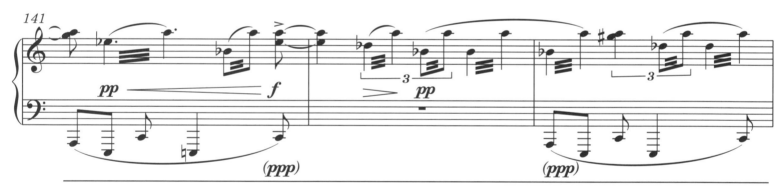

tremolo:
slow - fast - slow

rit.

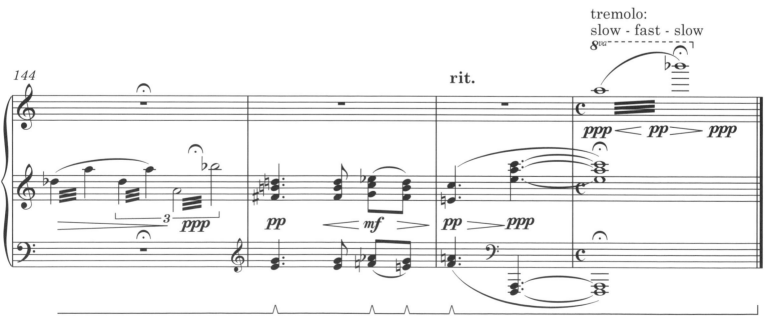

*Blank
for turn*

II. Shadows

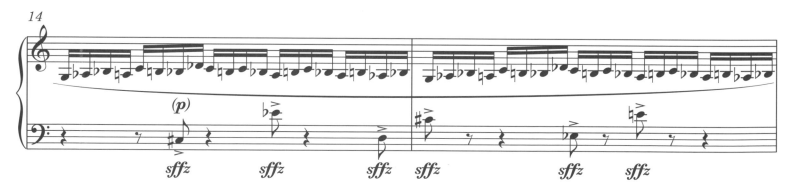

*All glissandi are white notes.

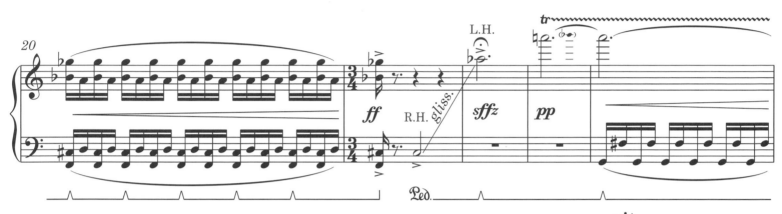

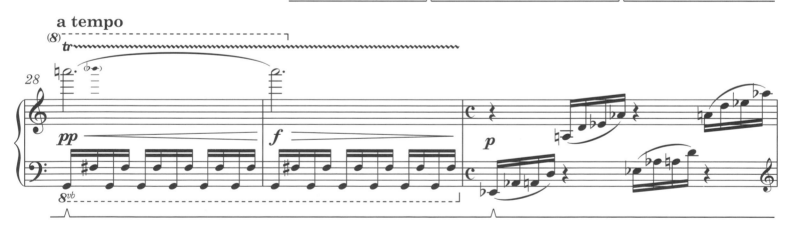

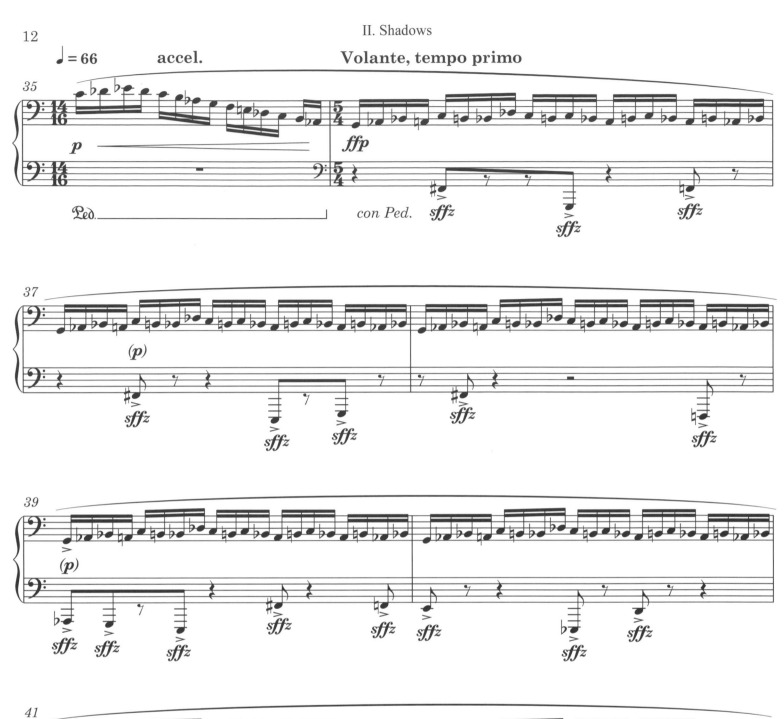

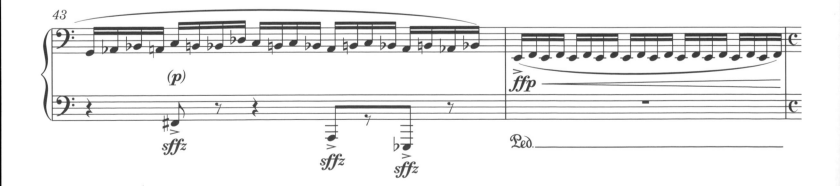

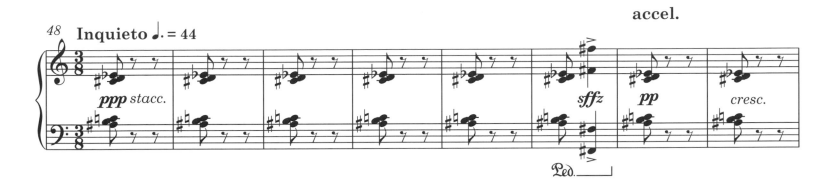

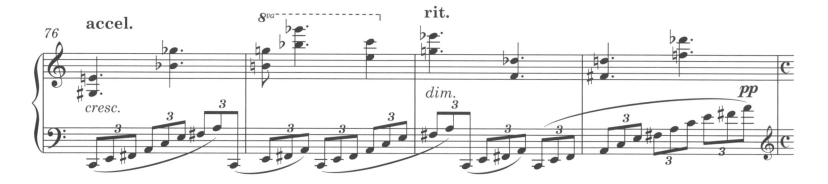

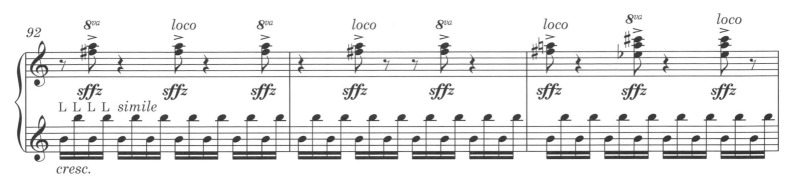

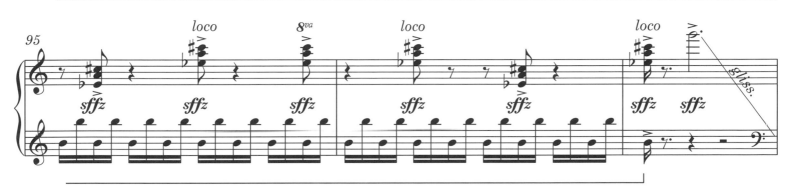

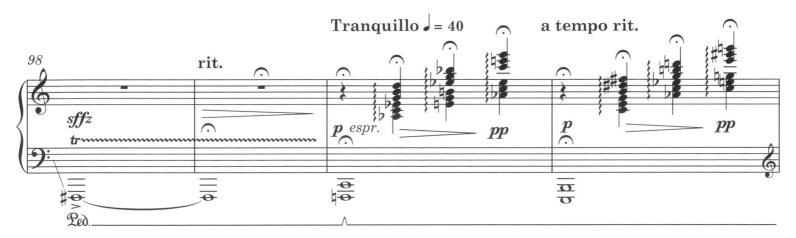

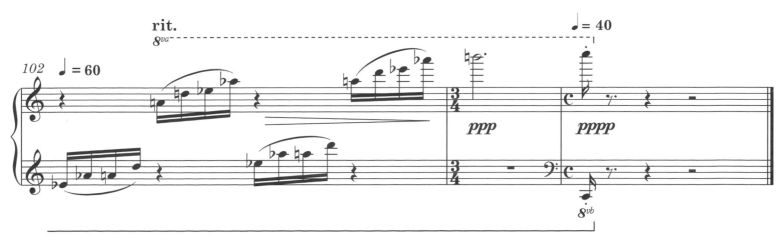

III. Light

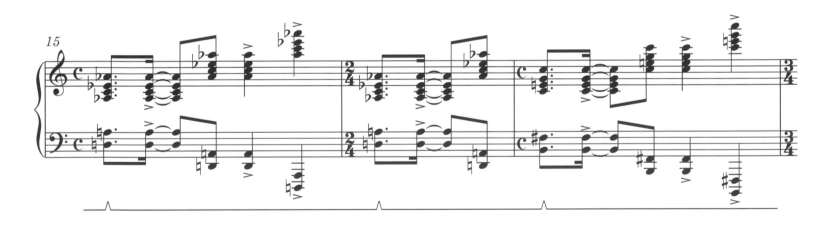

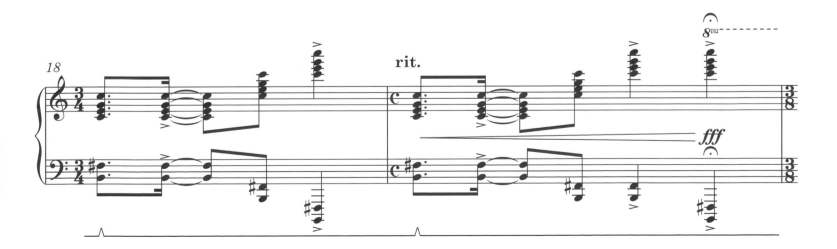

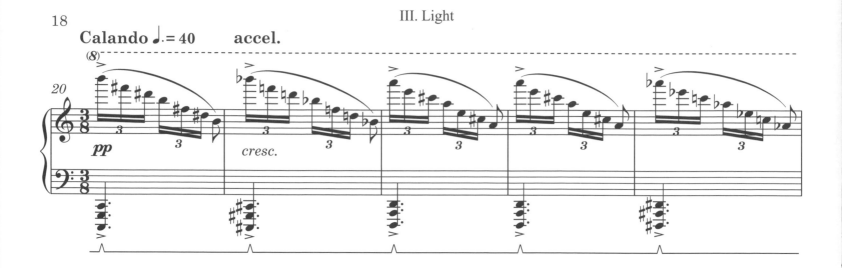

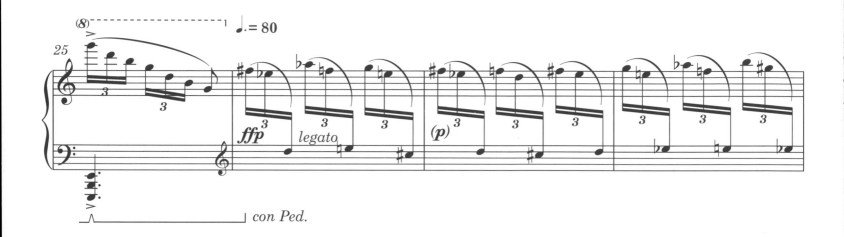

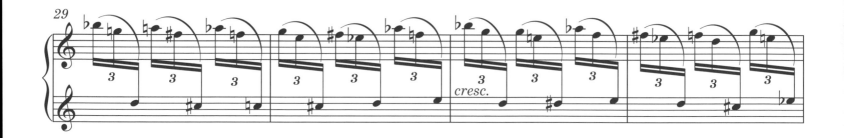

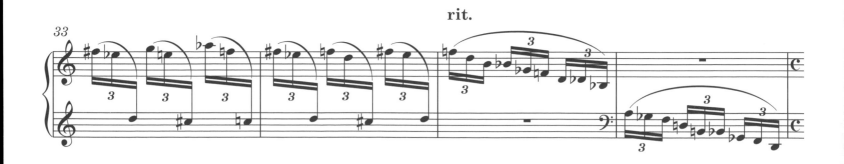

Tempo primo

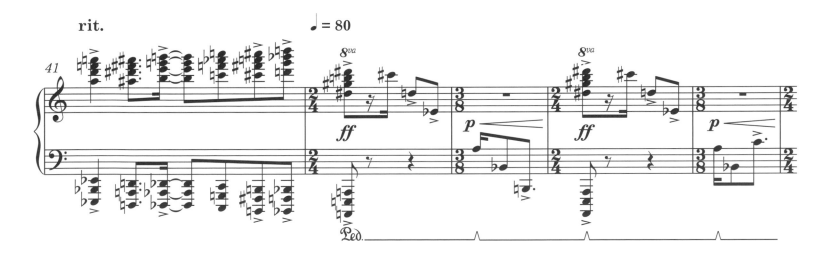

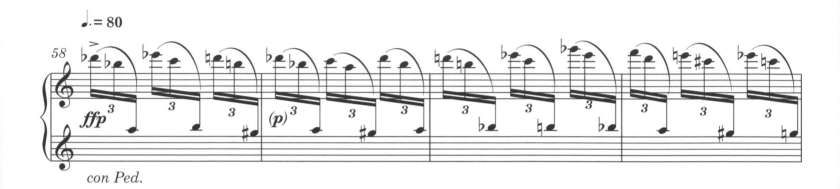

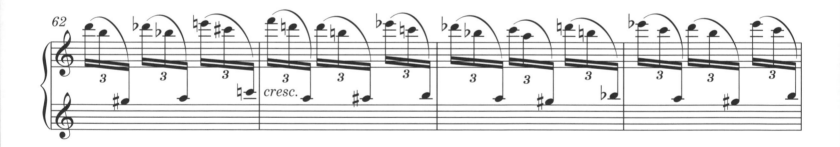

Tempo primo

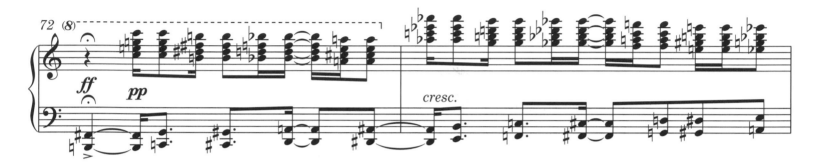

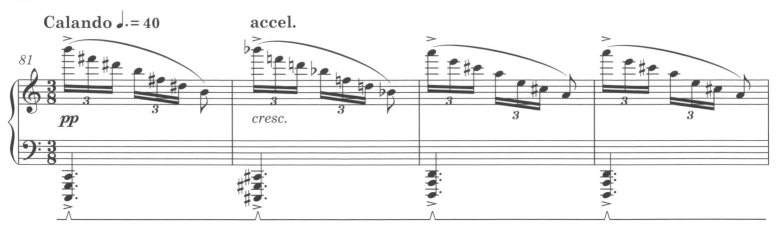

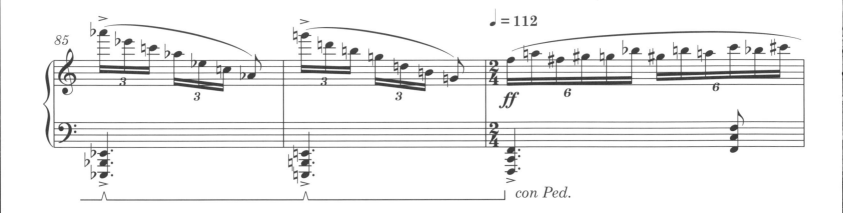

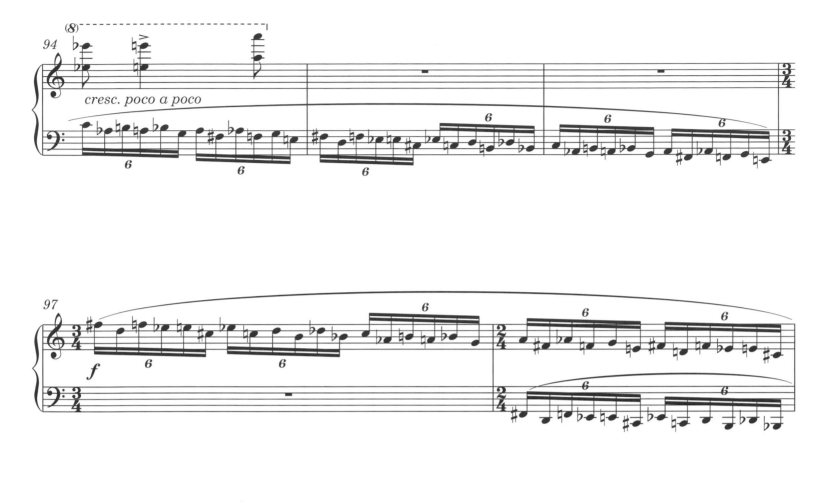

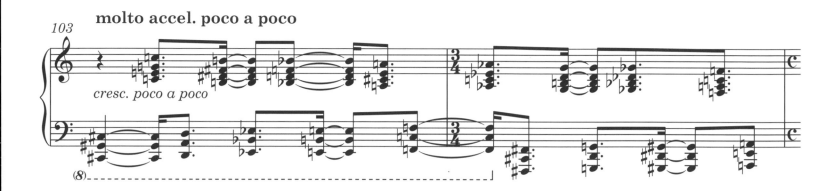

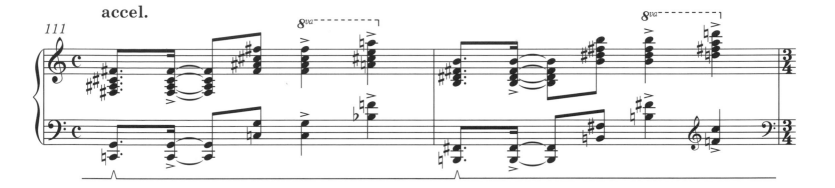

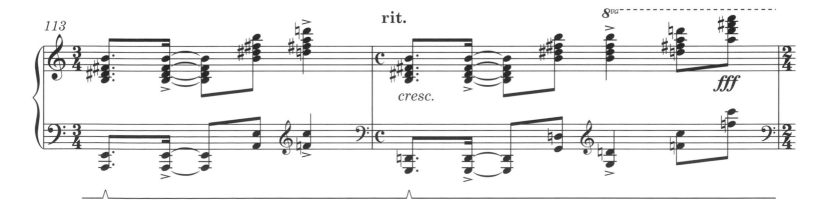

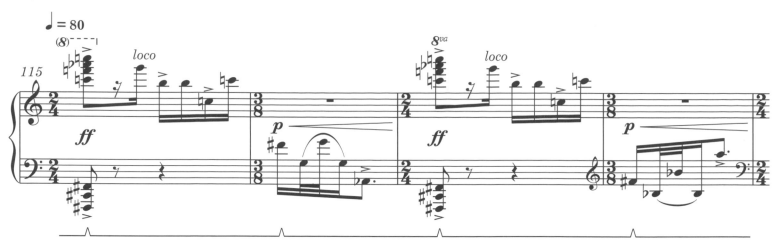

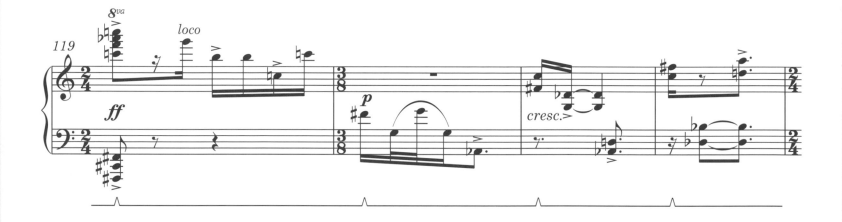

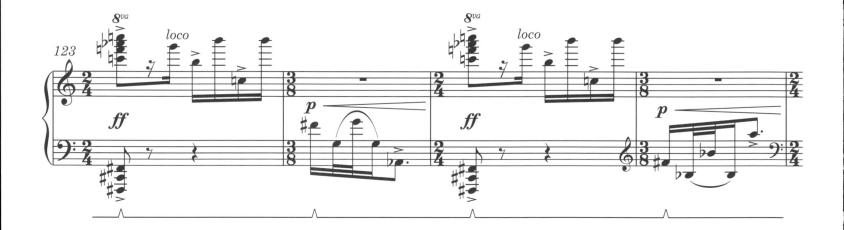

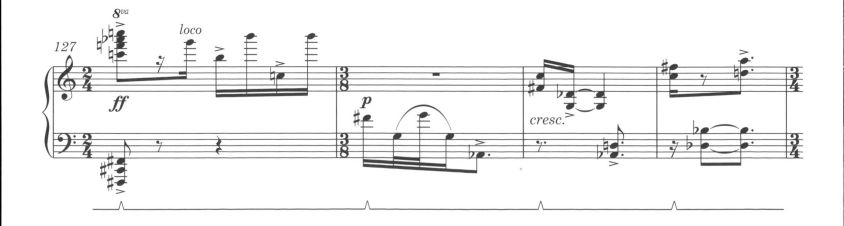

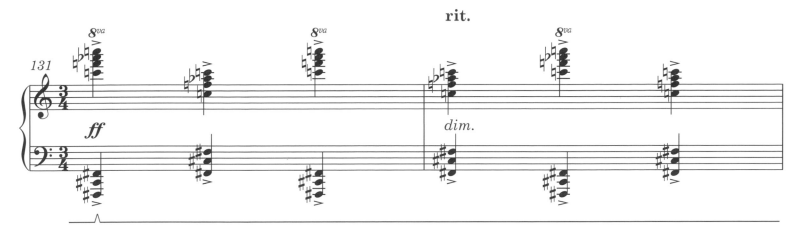

rit.

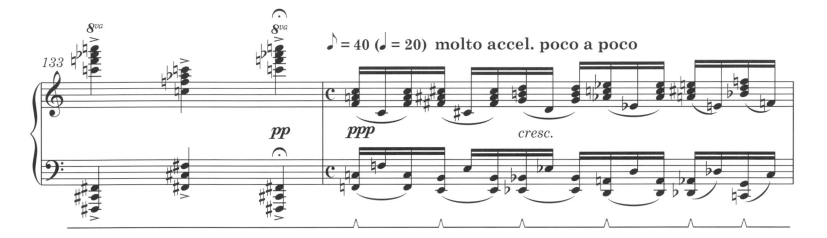

♪ = 40 (♩ = 20) molto accel. poco a poco

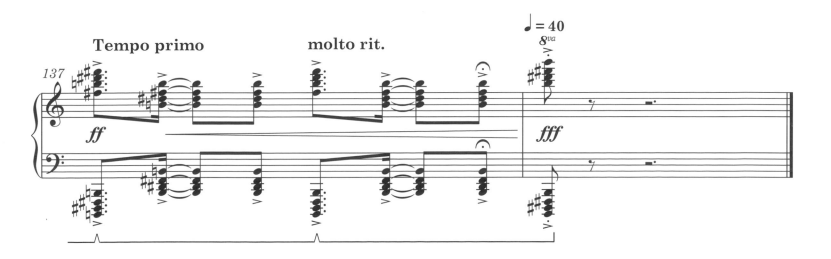

Tempo primo

molto rit.

♩ = 40